Measure Up!

SPEED

Navin Sullivan

Marshall Cavendish
Benchmark
New York

Marshall Cavendish Benchmark
99 White Plains Road
Tarrytown, New York 10591
www.marshallcavendish.us

Library of Congress Cataloging-in-Publication Data

Sullivan, Navin.
  Speed / by Navin Sullivan.
     p. cm. — (Measure up!)
  Summary: "Discusses speed, the science behind measuring speed, and the different devices used to measure speed"—Provided by publisher.
  Includes bibliographical references and index.
  ISBN-13: 978-0-7614-2325-6
  ISBN-10: 0-7614-2325-7
  1. Speed—Juvenile literature. 2. Acceleration (Mechanics)—Juvenile literature. 3. Mensuration—Juvenile literature. I. Title. II. Series.

  QC137.52.S86 2007
  531'.112--dc22
  2006020929

  QC256.S85 2007
  536'.5—dc22
  2006011981

Editor: Karen Ang
Editorial Director: Michelle Bisson
Art Director: Anahid Hamparian
Series Designer: Alex Ferrari

Photo Research by Iain Morrison

Cover: Digital Vision Ltd. / SuperStock

The photographs in this book are used by permission and through the courtesy of: *Corbis*: Gerolf Kalt/Zefa, 4; Royalty Free, 7; Reuters, 1, 9; Mark E. Gibson, 10; Jim Sugar, 12; Robert Sciarrino/Star Ledger, 17; Bowe Christy/Sygma, 18; Daniel Ramsbott/EPA, 22; Bettmann, 25, 31, 41; Rob Howard, 32; Ariel Skelley, 34; NASA, 36; Mike Theiss/Jim Reed Photography, 38. *The Image Works*: SSPL, 13, 35, 40. *Photo Researchers, Inc.*: John Beatty, 16; Stephen J. Krasemann, 20 (top and bottom); Royal Observatory, Edinburgh, 27; Detler Van Ravenswaay, 29.

Printed in China
1 3 5 6 4 2

Contents

Once they are cruising in the air, most commercial jets travel at a speed of about 500 miles per hour. If they did not travel at such fast speeds, they would be unable to stay in the air.

CHAPTER ONE

What Is Speed?

What is the fastest speed you have ever traveled? Maybe 55 miles per hour in a car, or even more in a commuter train. If you have flown in a jumbo jet, you will have traveled at a speed of about 500 miles per hour.

When you are riding in a plane, you may not feel like you are moving fast, but you are. An airplane can carry you a long way in a short time. That is because it moves at a high speed. In most cases, the faster or higher a speed is, the less time it takes to cross a distance. An object's speed is measured by the distance traveled divided by the time it took to cross the distance. The formula looks like this:

$$\textbf{Speed = Distance} \div \textbf{Time}$$

Speed is often measured as distance in miles divided by time in hours. So one mile per hour (or 1 mph) is a unit measure of speed. However, other units can also be used. To measure something slow, you might use millimeters per minute or inches per hour. You choose the units that suit your purpose. For example, if a snail takes nearly 2-$\frac{1}{2}$ days to travel 100 yards, what units would you choose for measuring its speed? You probably would not choose miles per hour. Since you know that the snail travels a certain number of yards in a specific number of days, you could measure its speed in yards per day (yards/day). By using the formula (Distance ÷ Time = Speed) you can determine that the snail moves 40 yards in one day:

100 yards ÷ 2-1/2 days = 40 yards per day

How can you take it one step further and figure out the snail's speed in yards per hour? There are 24 hours in one day. So to figure out the snail's speed in yards per hour you would use the basic speed formula and make hours your unit of time:

40 yards ÷ 24 hours = 1.67 yards per hour

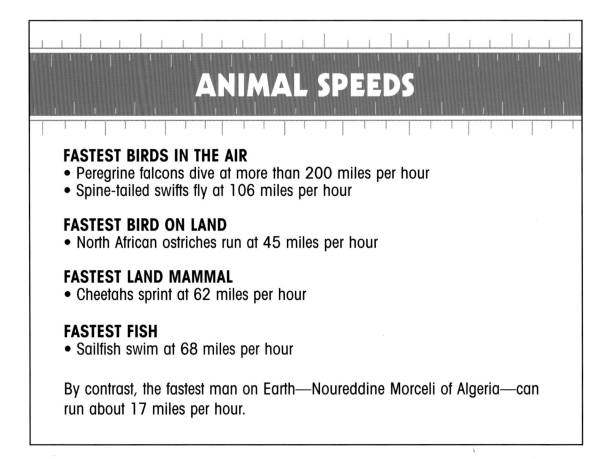

ANIMAL SPEEDS

FASTEST BIRDS IN THE AIR
• Peregrine falcons dive at more than 200 miles per hour
• Spine-tailed swifts fly at 106 miles per hour

FASTEST BIRD ON LAND
• North African ostriches run at 45 miles per hour

FASTEST LAND MAMMAL
• Cheetahs sprint at 62 miles per hour

FASTEST FISH
• Sailfish swim at 68 miles per hour

By contrast, the fastest man on Earth—Noureddine Morceli of Algeria—can run about 17 miles per hour.

AVERAGE SPEED

The speed at which something travels may vary during the course of a trip. When you ride in a car, the driver may slow down in heavy traffic or for lower speed-limit zones. An airplane goes more slowly when climbing or descending than when cruising high up in the air. These differences affect the overall speed. In order to account for this, average speed is used. Average speed is the total distance traveled divided by the total time it took to go from beginning to end. As an equation, we write this as:

Average Speed =
Distance ÷ Total Time

Speed limits can vary from area to area, depending upon things such as winding roads or school zones. Outside of the United States, speed limits are usually posted using metric measurements—such as kilometers per hour—instead of miles per hour.

Average speed is always less than the highest speed achieved and is always more than the slowest speed. For example, an airplane may go at 600 mph when traveling at 35,000 feet above the earth, but when it climbs into the sky or descends it probably travels at 300 mph. Therefore, the plane's average speed has to be somewhere between 300 mph and 600 mph.

The equation or formula for average speed can also be used to figure out journey times. You can turn around the equation for average speed and write:

Journey Time = Distance ÷ Average Speed

Knowing the distance to be covered, and assuming an average speed, you can use the equation to find the likely journey time. For example, suppose you live 300 miles away from

AVERAGE SPEED

In 1776 patriot John Adams went to Philadelphia to help write the Declaration of Independence. He rode there from Quincy, Massachusetts, in a week. If you assume the distance from Philadelphia to Quincy is 322 miles and that he rode 10 hours a day, how would you calculate his average speed in miles per hour?

You know that he rode a total of 322 miles in 7 days. So each day he rode 46 miles (322 ÷ 7 = 46).

Each day he rode for 10 hours. So his average speed is equal to the distance divided by the total time:

46 miles ÷ 10 hours = 4.6 miles per hour

The average speed of Adams's horse was 4.6 miles per hour.

Boston, Massachusetts, and want to go there by car. How long will it take? You can assume that the driver knows the route and will achieve an average speed of 50 mph.

300 miles ÷ 50 miles per hour = 6 hours

Assuming you do not get lost, and the average speed remains about the same, your trip should only take you six hours.

VELOCITY

Velocity combines speed with a definite direction. Anything that is moving in a definite direction has a specific velocity. The formula for figuring out speed still applies, but you need to add a direction (north, south, east, west) to determine velocity. Fly due north at 500 mph and your velocity is 500 mph north.

Velocity is important when an object must travel at a certain speed in a specific direction. When testing missiles or other weapons, the military needs to know where the object is going and—based on its speed—when it will arrive.

Simple stopwatches are usually used during school races. Once you know how long it takes you to run a certain distance, you can usually figure out your speed.

CHAPTER TWO
Measuring Speed

MEASURING SPEED IN SPORTS

How would you time someone running the 100-yard dash? You would probably use a stopwatch and your eyesight. But what about a longer race, in which you cannot see both the beginning and the end of the race? You would then need another person to help you. Both of you would have synchronized watches, which are watches that are set to the same exact time. One of you would record the start time and the other would record the time when the first runner crossed the finish line.

In professional races, **photoelectric cells** provide the eyesight and the timing. At the start and finish lines a beam of light crosses the track. The light activates a photoelectric cell that converts the light into an electric current. When a runner interrupts the beam (when he or she crosses the line), the current stops. The times when this happens are recorded by the device. Often, a camera is also needed to record who crossed over the finish line and at what time.

MEASURING CAR SPEED

When you are in a moving car, how do you check your speed? You look at the **speedometer**, which is located on the dashboard in front of the steering wheel. A cable runs from inside the speedometer to the driveshaft in the engine. This driveshaft turns the wheels and makes the car move. The faster the shaft turns, the faster the wheels turn, and the faster you travel. As the shaft turns, the cable twirls around itself in time with the turning shaft. Inside the speedometer, the speed at which the cable twirls is translated into a display of the car's speed.

MEASURING AIRPLANE SPEED

Like a car, an airplane also measures its own speed as it travels. It carries a tube first devised in 1732 by a Frenchman, Henri Pitot. He used it to measure water pressure. Now it is used to measure air pressure, and from that, the speed of a plane.

An airplane's **Pitot tube** has its front end open to the air. During flight, as the airplane rushes forward, the tube is filled with air

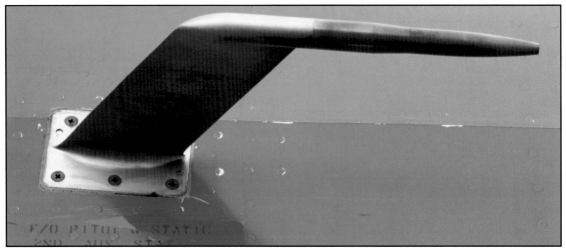

Pitot tubes come in many forms, depending upon the aircraft. Some pitot tubes have special coverings that protect them from the weather or dirt, dust, or other materials in the air.

that is forced into it. As a result, the air pressure in the tube goes up. The faster the airplane is traveling, the higher the air pressure in the tube will be. This pressure is compared with the pressure in the baggage compartment in the airplane, called the hold. The difference in pressures indicates the speed of the plane. This speed can be displayed on a dial like a speedometer needle or, in modern airplanes, in digital form. Most planes have an extra mechanism that shows the maximum allowable speed for that particular plane. This warns the pilot if the plane is going too fast.

MEASURING WIND SPEED

Wind speed and direction offers an indication of what the weather is going to be like. Measuring the wind's speed can help people make important decisions. For example, if gale force winds of 40 mph are expected, sailors of small boats know that they should stay on shore.

The person who forecasts the weather, called a meteorologist, measures wind speed with an **anemometer**. This device

This four-cup anemometer was made in 1846.

By following these directions, you can make your own anemometer.

Materials:
Four small paper drinking cups
Two 1-foot strips of cardboard (for example, from a cereal box)
A ruler
A stapler
A push pin or thumbtack
A pencil with an eraser on top
Modeling clay
A watch
A marker

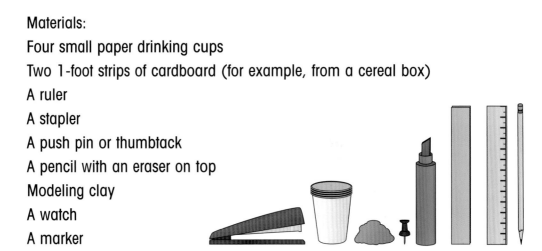

Color the rim—or just a part—of one cup with the marker. Place the cardboard strips together so that the middle of one crosses the middle of the other. Staple the two strips together. You should now have a cross with four equal arms—each arm should be 6-inches long.

Staple each cup through its side, underneath the end of each cardboard strip. Make sure the cups are horizontal.

Push the pin or thumbtack through the center of the crossed cardboard and into the eraser of the pencil. Hold the pencil upright and blow into the cups to check if they spin around freely.

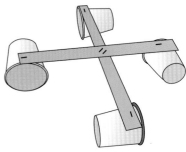

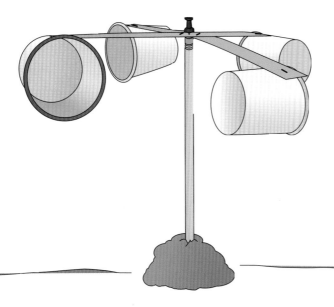

You have now made a wind speed indicator. Next, you need to test it. Put a lump of modeling clay on a flat surface outdoors. Holding the pencil upright, push the sharpened point of the pencil deep into the clay to anchor it firmly. Wait for a breeze. As the arms revolve, count how many times the colored cup spins around in a minute.

To use your indicator, you need to know how fast it turns at different wind speeds. Get local wind speeds each day from your local weather forecast. Note the turns per minute for different wind speeds. After you have done this for about a week, you should have a pretty good idea of how well your anemometer is indicating wind speed.

Some anemometers are small enough to be used by hand. This scientist is measuring the wind speed in Antarctica.

has three or four cups on arms joined to a vertical metal pole. When the wind blows against the cups, the wind pressure on the cups makes the pole turn around. The pole is connected to a tiny electric generator. As the pole turns, it makes the generator produce a continuous electric current. The faster the pole turns, the greater the current will be. The strength of the current is converted into a wind speed that a meteorologist can record.

MEASURING SPEED BY RADAR

Some high-frequency radio waves are called **radar waves**. These waves move up and down, like the waves on the ocean. The distance between two of the waves' peaks (that are next to each other) is called the **wavelength**. Radar waves travel at 186,000 miles per second, which means that they are practically instantaneous. The waves make a narrow beam that is reflected by any object in their path. The time it takes for the waves to go out from the radar source, hit an object, and return gives the object's distance. If the waves are stretched out on their return, the object is moving away from the radar source. If the waves are closer together when they return, the object is approaching. Differences in the wavelength show how fast the object is approaching or receding (moving away).

Car drivers exceeding the speed limit are easily tracked by police officers who use radar. Because radar waves travel through fog, airport controllers can monitor an incoming airplane by radar even

A police officer uses a radar gun to track the speeds of oncoming cars.

The board behind Andre Agassi shows the speed of the tennis ball coming his way. Agassi is moving his racket at such a fast speed that the camera could not catch it—it almost looks invisible.

when weather conditions cause poor visibility. Meteorologists use radar for tracking dense air in storms. The dense air can indicate whether or not a storm will improve or will worsen.

Radar can also be used in some sports. For example, in tennis matches, the speed at which a tennis ball is served is measured through radar. During major professional matches, the speed of the serve is usually displayed behind the players. Two of the fastest recorded speeds are a man's serve at 127 mph and a woman's at 119 mph.

REACTION SPEED

What do we mean when we talk about someone having quick or slow reactions? Often, we are talking about sports, in which an athlete responds quickly to a ball thrown his or her way. Reaction speeds are sometimes called reflexes, or how quickly you respond to something. To be able to react quickly is very useful. If you are in a car in heavy traffic and the car in front suddenly brakes, your driver needs to react quickly to avoid a collision.

Some reactions, or reflexes, are natural. Have you ever had a doctor lightly tap your knee with a special instrument during an exam? If the doctor hits the right place, your leg should kick out in response. The doctor is testing your reflexes. Those kind of reflexes are involuntary, which means your body should automatically do them. The doctor is checking to see how quickly your body reacts to the tap. If your

Animals are not the only living things with quick reaction speeds. Some plants react quickly to their environment. This sensitive mimosa plant (above) closes its leaves when it is touched (below). This reaction happens in under a second.

body's reaction speed is too slow, your doctor might want to perform more tests to make sure there is nothing wrong.

Many animals react much more quickly than we do. Have you ever had a cat scratch you before you even realized it? Animals like cats have much faster reaction times than humans. The cat sensed your presence, decided that it needed to scratch you, and did it all in an instant. By the time you see its moving paw you have already been scratched.

TESTING REACTION SPEEDS

You will need a ruler and a friend or classmate to help you perform this experiment. Ask your friend to hold the ruler vertically. Make sure the ruler is held so that the smallest measurement is on the bottom. Place your pointer (or index) finger and thumb on either side of the bottom of the ruler. (Your fingers should be positioned so that if you were to pinch your fingers together, you would be holding the flat sides of the ruler.) Hold your fingers about about 1/2 an inch apart, and get ready.

Have your friend release the ruler without warning. Try to catch it with your pointer and thumb. How far it falls before you catch it indicates your reaction time. How many inches does the ruler fall before you catch it? After doing it a few times, does your reaction speed improve or stay the same? Trade places and let your friend try catching the ruler. Which of you is faster?

When they first jump out of a plane, skydivers are moving through the air at very fast speeds. However, once they open their parachutes, they slow down and can usually direct their landing.

CHAPTER THREE

Speed and Gravity

ACCELERATION

An increase in speed is called acceleration. When a car pulls away from the curb, the driver accelerates to get up to normal driving speed. The driver usually increases speed rapidly until the car is doing 30 mph. Then the driver probably decreases the amount of acceleration, so the car increases speed more slowly as it moves up to 40 mph or 50 mph. The acceleration, or increase in speed, is greater at the beginning, even though the actual speed is lower at the beginning than it is later on.

At the end of the journey the driver does the opposite of accelerating, which is decelerating. The driver decelerates to slow the car down. At first, the **deceleration** may be rapid, to slow the car in a short time from 50 mph to 30 mph. Then the deceleration may be less. That means that the car's speed decreases from 30 mph to 10 mph over a longer period of time.

ACCELERATION DUE TO GRAVITY

Things fall to Earth because the planet exerts an attractive force called **gravity** that pulls them. Around 1630, an Italian scientist,

Galileo Galilei, wanted to measure the strength of this force. He dropped a heavy iron ball from a high tower and tried to estimate how long it took the ball to fall to Earth. However, Galileo lived in the days before stopwatches, and the ball fell too rapidly for him to time how long it took to fall.

He had to measure the pull of gravity some other way. He decided to try lessening the effect of gravity by rolling a ball down a slope. That way, the ball would not move as fast as when it was falling straight down. He made a long straight channel of polished wood. Along the side he marked distances. Then he set it at a slope. He put a polished bronze ball in the channel at the top and let it roll down. To time the different positions that the ball reached at each second, he set up a simple device containing water that ran out at a standard rate per second.

Each second, the ball traveled farther than in the previous second. This meant that its speed was increasing each second. The ball was accelerating. Suppose that in the first second it traveled 1 foot down the channel. In the next second it traveled 3 feet. In the third second it traveled 5 feet. In the fourth second it went 7 feet. The ball traveled farther every second, and was, therefore, moving faster every second. However, the rate of its change in speed, or its acceleration, remained the same all through the experiment. Its acceleration was constant.

Next, he tried increasing the slope of the channel and timing the ball again. With a steeper slope, the ball rolled down faster, but its

FALLING FROM THE AIR

When skydivers drop from an airplane high up in the air, without opening their parachutes, they begin accelerating downward. However, after they have fallen a while they stop accelerating, and maintain a steady speed of about 140 mph. The reason for this is that at that speed the air cannot part quickly enough and cushions the skydivers' fall.

If they began to fall above Earth's atmosphere the results would be different. In 1960 Captain Joe Kittinger of the U.S. Air Force dropped from a balloon way above the atmosphere. He fell from an altitude of 102,200 feet to 17,500 feet before opening his parachute. By then he was falling at 614 mph.

Captain Kittinger makes his historic jump in 1960.

acceleration was the same as before. The same was true with every slope he tried.

Eventually Galileo calculated the acceleration as an increase in speed every second of 32 feet per second. He realized that this would still be true if the wooden channel were vertical—in other words, if the ball was falling freely. This, then, was the acceleration due to gravity.

He tried experimenting with different-sized balls, and always got the same result. He may have also tried dropping objects of different weights from the top of his tower. If he had, he would have found that they all hit the ground at the same time.

Through his experiments, Galileo proved that everything falls with the same acceleration. The Greek scientist Aristotle, around 350 BCE, had thought that a heavy ball would fall faster than a lighter one. However, he only supposed this—he did not test his hunch. If he had done a simple scientific experiment he would have been proven wrong. Light and heavy objects fall with the same acceleration. Their final speed only depends on how long they have been falling and accelerating.

SATELLITES

In 1686, the British scientist, Sir Isaac Newton, experimented with laws of motion by using logic and mathematics. One law stated that moving objects keep going unless some force stops them. They do not stop because their speed is somehow used up. When you roll a ball across a flat grassy yard, it slows down and eventually stops because the grass prevents it from moving freely.

Hurl a ball upward into the air, and it gradually slows, stops going up, and begins falling. This is because the force of your throw competes with the force of gravity. Eventually, gravity wins.

Can you imagine throwing a ball so fast that it would not come down? Newton did. He considered what would happen if he fired a cannon from the top of a mountain. The cannon ball would go a mile or so, but gravity would bring it down. If the cannon were more powerful, the ball would go farther, but still eventually fall.

Newton then asked himself what would happen if the ball were fired from a super-cannon. If the ball traveled with enough

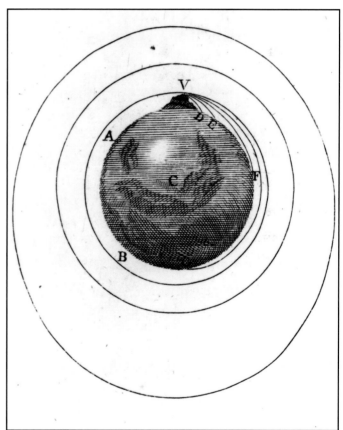

This gravity map by Newton shows how an object launched from a high mountain (V) would orbit around the planet at different velocities. At lower velocities (D, E, F, G), an object would not travel far before crashing back to Earth. High velocities (A, B and the outer rings) are needed for an object to stay in orbit.

force to equal the pull of gravity, the ball would neither go farther up nor come down. Instead, it would keep going at the same height above the ground. What would be the result? The ball would travel around Earth, held in its **orbit** by gravity. Assuming that there was no air resistance to slow it (the way grass slows a rolling ball), it would keep going around Earth forever!

Without knowing it, Newton had anticipated the creation of artificial satellites. The first man-made satellite, *Sputnik I*, was put into orbit by the Soviet Union in 1957, almost 300 years later.

ORBITAL VELOCITY

The pull of Earth's gravity decreases the farther away you are from Earth's center. The force that Galileo measured was at **sea level**, which is 4,000 miles from the center. If he had measured gravity at twice that distance (8,000 miles) from the center, the pull would have been a quarter as strong. At three times that distance (12,000 miles), the pull of gravity is one-ninth of what it would be at Earth's center. If you are four times (16,000 miles) as far away from the center, its pull is one-sixteenth. The pull lessens in proportion to the distance multiplied by itself, which is called the square of the distance. Therefore, at twice the distance the pull is four times weaker (2 x 2 = 4). At three times the distance the pull is only one ninth as strong (3 x 3 = 9). At four times the distance the pull is only one sixteenth as strong (4 x 4 = 16).

Keeping a satellite in orbit is a neat balancing act. It must be inserted into orbit at a speed that balances gravitational pull. The higher the orbit of the satellite, the less the pull of gravity on the satellite will be. As a result, a lower speed is needed to keep it in orbit. High above the atmosphere, at 143 miles above sea level, a satellite must go 12,000 mph to stay in orbit. Traveling twelve times faster than

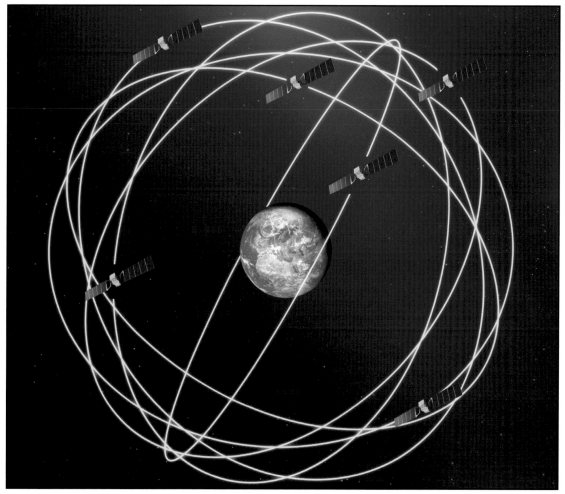

This computer artwork shows how multiple satellites can orbit the planet at the same time. However, when launching the satellites, different velocities are needed for each satellite so that their orbits will not interfere with each other.

the rotating Earth, which at the equator rotates at 1,000 mph, the satellite goes once around Earth every two hours.

At an altitude of 22,370 miles gravity is only 1/30 of what it is at sea level. A satellite going 1,000 mph stays in orbit and matches the speed of the turning Earth. From the ground it appears stationary. It is said to be in **geostationary orbit**.

ESCAPE VELOCITY

As a rocket climbs, gravity's pull on it lessens dramatically. If a rocket blasts off at 6.5 miles per second (6.5 mps), it will climb to 25,800 miles before falling to Earth. At that altitude the pull is only 1/40 of what it would be at sea level. If the rocket climbs at 6.6 mps it will climb to 34,300 miles before falling. If it climbs at 6.98 mps it will never fall at all! It will go onward into space. This speed is called the **escape velocity**.

Escaping from a big planet is more difficult than from a small one, because the gravitational pull from a big planet is greater than that from a small one. To blast off from the Moon a space vehicle needs an escape velocity of only 1.5 mps. To escape from Mars, it would need 3.2 mps. From Saturn the vehicle would need 23 mps. Jupiter, the most massive planet in our solar system, requires an escape velocity of 38 mps—nearly 5-1/2 times Earth's escape velocity!

Scientists need to calculate escape velocity before a space shuttle is launched.

If you look carefully while someone is playing a drum, you can see the skin vibrate in time. These vibrations send out very fast sound waves.

CHAPTER FOUR

The Speed of Sound

SOUND WAVES

Have you ever watched a drummer playing in a band? As the drummer beats the skin of the drum, the skin vibrates up and down. Every time the skin goes up, it pushes the air above the drum, making a wave of moving air. This wave of moving air **compresses** the air ahead of it. You can see the vibrations of the drum skin, but not the compressions in the air. The invisible compressions in the air travel to our ears. In your ear there is another little skin, called the ear drum. When the compressions hit it, your ear drum vibrates the same way as the drum skin. You then hear the wave as the sound from the drum.

You can see the **taut** strings in violins, guitars, or pianos vibrate as they are played. Like the skin of the drum, these strings send out air compressions. However, the pattern of air compressions that they make is more complicated than the pattern from the drum skin. Each string can make different sounds. Also, altering the length of the string being used changes the **pitch** of the sound coming from that string. Notes from short strings are higher than those from long strings.

Wind instruments such as the flute or saxophone contain air.

Using your fingers to shorten or lengthen the strings of an instrument will alter the sound waves.

When they are played, the air inside them vibrates. The vibrations travel as compression waves to your ears. Altering the length of air used alters the sound.

Clap your hands together, and you compress the air between them. You then hear that compression as your clap. A tornado going across the Midwest at 150 mph generates great compression waves. You can hear these waves as a deep rumbling noise.

SPEED OF SOUND

In 1832, two researchers in Holland, Moll and Van Beek, set up two cannons on hills 11 miles apart. When night fell, the cannon on one hill was fired. On the other hill, observers saw the flash of gunpowder, and later heard the noise of the exploding gunpowder. They timed the difference between the flash and the noise. The time between the light and the sound was the time it took for sound to travel 11 miles. To check their results and to cancel the effect of any wind, they then fired the other cannon in the opposite direction. The combined result was 750 mph, which was very close to today's figure of 740 mph at sea level in freezing cold air.

The speed of sound in air varies with altitude. The atmosphere becomes thinner the higher you go above sea level. In thin air, it takes longer for the waves of sound to compress the air, and so the sound travels more slowly. The speed of sound also varies with the air temperature. When air is warm, it is thinner than when it is cold. So sound travels more slowly through warm air than through cold air. Sound waves need a solid, a liquid, or air to carry them. They cannot travel in a **vacuum** or through space because there is no air to carry the waves.

SUPERSONIC FLIGHT

Supersonic aircraft can fly faster than the speed of sound. Their speed is measured by a Mach number, named after Ernst Mach, an Austrian physicist who lived in the 1800s. **Mach 1** is defined as the speed of sound at a particular altitude and temperature. The higher the

Through his experiments, Ernst Mach was able to relate the speed of sound to local air temperatures and pressures.

altitude, or the higher the temperature, the slower the sound and the lower the value of Mach 1.

At speeds above Mach 1 an airplane is going faster than sound at that particular altitude and temperature. Air cannot move out of the airplane's way fast enough. Instead, the airplane compresses the air, making it difficult to fly through it. The airplane has to batter its way upward through this wall of compressed air. This wall is called the **sound barrier**. When a plane travels this fast, a wave of compressed air follows the airplane. This wave spreads downward and people on the ground hear it as a sharp crack after the airplane has passed overhead. The shock wave may even break windows in buildings under the airplane's flight path. An airplane flying at supersonic speeds has to fly as high as possible where the air is very thin and the sound barrier is easier to break through.

The fastest commercial airplane to fly above Mach 2 (twice the

Scientists are trying to develop hypersonic aircraft. These jets will travel above Mach 5—or more than five times faster than the speed of sound.

local speed of sound) was the Anglo-French Concorde. It was only allowed to fly over the oceans because its speed kept breaking glass in buildings below it. The Concorde took only 3-$\frac{1}{2}$ hours to fly the 3,300 miles from London, England, to New York, so its passengers could cross the Atlantic, spend part of the day there, and then return all in the same day. Many military aircraft fly faster than Mach 2 when they are on duty.

SOUND IN SOLIDS

Sound waves move faster through solids than air. Solids are closely packed together and transmit the waves more quickly. It has been said that some Native Americans used to put their ears to the ground to be aware of when their enemies were approaching. From the sounds they could estimate whether there were many people approaching, or only a few. This enabled them to be prepared and either retreat or to mount an offensive. It was their equivalent of an early warning system.

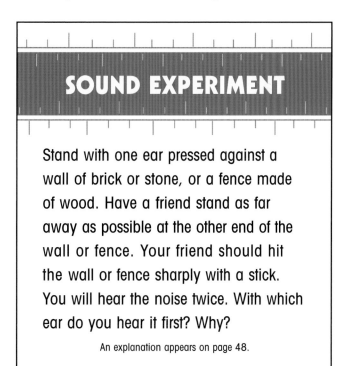

SOUND EXPERIMENT

Stand with one ear pressed against a wall of brick or stone, or a fence made of wood. Have a friend stand as far away as possible at the other end of the wall or fence. Your friend should hit the wall or fence sharply with a stick. You will hear the noise twice. With which ear do you hear it first? Why?

An explanation appears on page 48.

Because light travels faster than sound, you will hear the lightning's crack only after you see the lightning strike.

CHAPTER FIVE

The Speed of Light

Thunderstorms can be quite scary. The dark sky is lit by flashes of lightning. Following the lightning are great claps of thunder, sometimes sounding as though they are right overhead. You see the lightning before you hear the thunder. This is because light travels much faster than sound.

Have you ever stood outside your home and used a mirror to reflect sunlight onto one of its windows to attract attention? You see the light flash off the window as soon as you tilt the mirror. The sunlight has gone from your mirror to the window and back to your eyes, yet it seems like it takes no time at all. How would you measure the speed of something that travels that fast?

Over four centuries ago, Galileo was the first person to try. He stationed two men with lanterns on hilltops several miles apart. One man sent a flash of light to the other. The other had to flash back at once. Galileo hoped to measure the time it took between the two flashes in

THUNDER AND LIGHTNING

To get an estimate of how far away the center of a storm is, count the seconds between the flash of lightning and the sound of thunder. Divide that number by 5 and you have the approximate distance in miles.

order to calculate the speed of light. He failed, because light traveled too fast for him to measure its speed. The necessary measuring apparatus had not yet been invented.

MEASURING THE SPEED OF LIGHT

Hippolyte Fizeau, a French scientist, measured the speed of light in 1849. He aimed an intense beam of light at a rotating wheel that had rounded metal teeth projecting around the rim. This wheel was called a cogwheel. As he rotated the wheel, the gaps between the teeth let flashes of light through. These flashes of light went to a mirror at his father's house, nearly 5-1/2 miles away, where they were reflected. As the reflected light returned, it flashed between the teeth of the rotating cogwheel, and Fizeau saw it. The round trip for the light was 10.78 miles.

Fizeau cranked the cogwheel faster until he saw the shortest possible flash of light. This meant that light was then exiting through one gap and returning through the next. The cogwheel had 720 teeth and he

In 1849, Hippolyte Fizeau was the French physicist who first measured the speed of light.

rotated it 25 times per second. The time between one gap and the next was only 1/18,000 of a second. That was how long the light took to make its round trip of 10.78 miles. He calculated that the light was traveling at 194,000 miles per second!

A year later, another French scientist, Jean Foucault, improved on Fizeau's apparatus. Foucault used a revolving eight-sided mirror instead of a cogwheel. This broke the light into smaller flashes. The speed he got for light in air was 185,000 miles per second. He also found that light traveled more slowly through water than air.

The most accurate measurements were made by an American scientist, Albert

To test his theories on the speed of light, Albert Michelson used a long tube to reflect light between huge mirrors.

Michelson. He used the same method as Fizeau's but with better equipment. Michelson's beam of light from a high-intensity arc lamp was very bright. His mirrors were 22 miles apart, on Mount San Antonio and Mount Wilson, in California, to provide a longer distance for the light to travel. The rotating mirror used to break the light into the shortest possible flashes had eight sides and rotated 528 turns per second. In 1927, Michelson announced that light travels 186,175 miles per second.

Later he sent light through a sealed steel pipe 3 feet in diameter and 1 mile long. The beam of light was bounced off several mirrors as it went to one end and then back again, making its total journey 10 miles. With special pumps all the air was extracted from the tube, leaving a vacuum inside it. In this vacuum the light traveled even faster than in air. In all, 2,885 measurements were made and the final result chosen was 186,287.5 miles per second. This is the figure used today by scientists everywhere when they discuss the speed of light.

The speed of light is one of the most fundamental values in modern science. Knowing this speed enables scientists do things such as measuring the universe or splitting atoms to harness nuclear power. When describing Michelson, the famous scientist Albert Einstein once said that he was "one of the greatest artists in the world of scientific experimentation." Thanks to him—and countless other scientists and inventors—we now have a better understanding of speed.

GLOSSARY

acceleration—An increase in speed.

anemometer—An instrument used to measure wind speed.

atoms—The smallest unit of matter. Atoms are the building blocks of all matter.

compress—To press or squeeze together.

deceleration—A decrease in speed.

escape velocity—The speed an object needs in order to escape from an object's gravitational force.

geostationary orbit—An orbit—when viewed from Earth—that appears to be stationary, but is not.

gravity—A force that pulls things toward the center of the earth.

Mach 1—The speed of sound at a particular altitude and temperature.

nuclear power—Energy obtained by splitting atoms.

orbit—The circular or elliptical path an object—such as a satellite, planet, or moon—takes as it moves around another object.

orbital velocity—The speed an object needs in order to stay in orbit.

photoelectric cell—A device that converts light into an electric current that can be measured.

pitch—The level—high or low—of a sound.

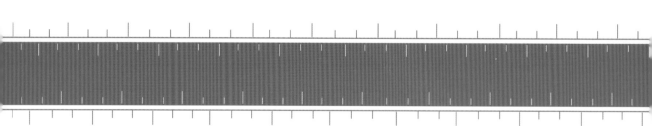

Pitot tube—A tube mounted on the outside of a plane, which uses air pressure to measure the plane's speed.

radar waves—Invisible, high-frequency radio waves.

sea level—The level of the ocean's surface. It is used to measure the depths of the oceans and land elevation or altitude.

sound barrier—The wall of compressed air through which an aircraft must pass in order to travel faster than the speed of sound.

speedometer—A device used to measure an object's—usually a vehicle's—speed.

supersonic—Describing something that travels above the speed of sound.

taut—To be drawn tight.

terminal velocity—The speed at which the force of gravity pulling on a falling object is equal to the amount of air resistance affecting that object. Once an object reaches this speed, it is no longer accelerating downward, and begins to fall at a constant speed.

vacuum—A space that is completely empty—there are no solids, liquids, or gases.

velocity—Measured speed in a definite direction, such as north, south, east, or west.

wavelength—The distance between two corresponding points on two waves that follow one another.

FIND OUT MORE

BOOKS

Farndon, John. *Motion.* Tarrytown, NY: Benchmark Books, 2003.

Gardner, Robert. *Split-Second Science Projects with Speed: How Fast Does It Go?* Berkeley Heights, NJ: Enslow Publishers, 2003.

Harris, Nicholas. *How Fast?* Farmington Hills, MI: Blackbirch Press, 2004.

WEB SITES

Speed Experiments for Students
http://www.acs.org/portal/a/c/s/1/wondernetdisplay.html?DOC=wondernet%5C
    grownups%5Cgu_speed.html

NASA's Space Place-Satellites in Orbit
http://spaceplace.nasa.gov/en/kids/goes/goes_poes_orbits.shtml

SEE IF YOU CAN ANSWER THESE PROBLEMS. YOU WILL NEED SOME NOTEBOOK PAPER TO WRITE YOUR EQUATIONS AND ANSWERS. FOR SOME OF THE PROBLEMS, YOU MIGHT NEED A CALCULATOR. ANSWERS TO THESE PROBLEMS ARE LOCATED ON PAGE 48.

CALCULATING SPEED

Speed = Distance ÷ Time
Average Speed = Distance ÷ Total Time

1. Assume that a person traveling at a constant speed can run 1 mile in 5 minutes. What is that person's speed in miles per hour?
2. Pretend that the person is able to run at that speed all day. What is his or her speed in miles per day?
3. A teacher needs to drive 770 miles to visit another school. He used his car for the trip, but needed to stop to buy gas and snacks. By the time he reached the other school, the trip took a total of 14 hours. What is the teacher's average speed for this trip?
4. An archer shoots an arrow toward a target that is located 30 feet north of her location. It takes the arrow 1 second to reach the target. What is the arrow's velocity?
5. Pretend that a super-arrow can continue to travel north at that speed for up to a minute. What is the super-arrow's velocity in feet per minute?

METRIC CONVERSIONS

To convert customary or standard units, such as feet or miles, into metric measurements, such as meters or kilometers, you can use these calculations:

1 foot = 0.3048 meters   — to change feet into meters, multiply by 0.3048
1 meter = 3.2808 feet   — to change meters into feet, multiply by 3.2809

1 mile = 1.6093 kilometers — to change miles into kilometers, multiply by 1.6093
1 kilometer = 0.6214 miles — to change kilometers into miles, multiply by 0.6214

1. If a plane is traveling 550 miles per hour, what is its speed in kilometers per hour?
2. An insect may crawl 3 yards in 1 minute. How many meters per minute is the insect traveling? (Remember, 1 yard = 3 feet.)

INDEX

PAGES NUMBERS FOR ILLUSTRATIONS ARE IN **BOLDFACE**

ANSWERS

Sidebar, page 37: The ear pressed to the wall or fence should hear the sound first. This is because sound travels through solids faster than through the air.

Page 46:

CALCULATING SPEED

1. That person can run 1/5 of a mile per minute (1 mile / 5 minutes = 1/5 miles per minute) and there are 60 minute in an hour. 1/5 x 60 = **12 miles per hour**
2. There are 24 hours in each day, so 12 miles per hour x 24 = **288 miles per day**
3. 770 miles ÷ 14 hours = an average speed of **55 miles per hour**
4. The target is 30 feet away and it takes the arrow 1 second to travel that far. The arrow's speed is 30 feet per second. But it is traveling in a northward direction, so the velocity is **30 feet per second north.**
5. There are 60 seconds in each minute, so 30 feet per second x 60 = 1,800 feet per minute. But the super-arrow is still traveling north, so the velocity is **1,800 feet per minute north.**

METRIC CONVERSIONS

1. 550 x 1.6093 = 885.115 kilometers. The plane travels at **885.115 kilometers per hour.**
2. The insect's speed is 3 yards per minute. Since there are 3 feet in every yard, 3 yards is equal to 9 feet (3 x 3 = 9).
1 foot = 0.3048 meters, so 9 feet x 0.3048 = 2.7432 meters
The insect's speed is **2.7432 meters per minute.**

ABOUT THE AUTHOR

Navin Sullivan has an M.A. in science from the University of Cambridge. He lives with his wife in London, England, and has dedicated many years to science education. He has edited various science texts, and has written science books for younger readers. Navin Sullivan has also been the CEO of a British educational publisher and Chairman of its Boston subsidiary. His hobbies include playing the piano and chess.

DATE DUE